# CONTENTS

# IDENTIFYING AMERICAN-MADE PRODUCTS

## HEARING

BEFORE THE

SUBCOMMITTEE ON
COMMERCE, CONSUMER PROTECTION, AND COMPETITIVENESS

OF THE

COMMITTEE ON
ENERGY AND COMMERCE
HOUSE OF REPRESENTATIVES

ONE HUNDRED THIRD CONGRESS

SECOND SESSION

ON

**H.R. 3342**

A BILL TO ESTABLISH A TOLL-FREE NUMBER IN THE DEPARTMENT OF COMMERCE TO ASSIST CONSUMERS IN DETERMINING IF PRODUCTS ARE AMERICAN-MADE

MAY 19, 1994

**Serial No. 103–132**

Printed for the use of the Committee on Energy and Commerce


U.S. GOVERNMENT PRINTING OFFICE

84-002CC WASHINGTON : 1994

For sale by the U.S. Government Printing Office
Superintendent of Documents, Congressional Sales Office, Washington, DC 20402
ISBN 0-16-046073-5

## COMMITTEE ON ENERGY AND COMMERCE

JOHN D. DINGELL, Michigan, *Chairman*

HENRY A. WAXMAN, California
PHILIP R. SHARP, Indiana
EDWARD J. MARKEY, Massachusetts
AL SWIFT, Washington
CARDISS COLLINS, Illinois
MIKE SYNAR, Oklahoma
W.J. "BILLY" TAUZIN, Louisiana
RON WYDEN, Oregon
RALPH M. HALL, Texas
BILL RICHARDSON, New Mexico
JIM SLATTERY, Kansas
JOHN BRYANT, Texas
RICK BOUCHER, Virginia
JIM COOPER, Tennessee
J. ROY ROWLAND, Georgia
THOMAS J. MANTON, New York
EDOLPHUS TOWNS, New York
GERRY E. STUDDS, Massachusetts
RICHARD H. LEHMAN, California
FRANK PALLONE, JR., New Jersey
CRAIG A. WASHINGTON, Texas
LYNN SCHENK, California
SHERROD BROWN, Ohio
MIKE KREIDLER, Washington
MARJORIE MARGOLIES-MEZVINSKY, Pennsylvania
BLANCHE M. LAMBERT, Arkansas

CARLOS J. MOORHEAD, California
THOMAS J. BLILEY, JR., Virginia
JACK FIELDS, Texas
MICHAEL G. OXLEY, Ohio
MICHAEL BILIRAKIS, Florida
DAN SCHAEFER, Colorado
JOE BARTON, Texas
ALEX MCMILLAN, North Carolina
J. DENNIS HASTERT, Illinois
FRED UPTON, Michigan
CLIFF STEARNS, Florida
BILL PAXON, New York
PAUL E. GILLMOR, Ohio
SCOTT KLUG, Wisconsin
GARY A. FRANKS, Connecticut
JAMES C. GREENWOOD, Pennsylvania
MICHAEL D. CRAPO, Idaho

ALAN J. ROTH, *Staff Director and Chief Counsel*
DENNIS B. FITZGIBBONS, *Deputy Staff Director*
MARGARET A. DURBIN, *Minority Chief Counsel and Staff Director*

---

## SUBCOMMITTEE ON COMMERCE, CONSUMER PROTECTION, AND COMPETITIVENESS

CARDISS COLLINS, Illinois, *Chairwoman*

EDOLPHUS TOWNS, New York
JIM SLATTERY, Kansas
J. ROY ROWLAND, Georgia
THOMAS J. MANTON, New York
RICHARD H. LEHMAN, California
FRANK PALLONE, JR., New Jersey
JOHN D. DINGELL, Michigan (Ex Officio)

CLIFF STEARNS, Florida
ALEX MCMILLAN, North Carolina
BILL PAXON, New York
JAMES C. GREENWOOD, Pennsylvania
CARLOS J. MOORHEAD, California (Ex Officio)

DAVID SCHOOLER, *Staff Director/Chief Counsel*
M. BRUCE GWINN, *Special Assistant*
DOUGLAS F. BENNETT, *Minority Counsel*

# IDENTIFYING AMERICAN-MADE PRODUCTS

---

**THURSDAY, MAY 19, 1994**

HOUSE OF REPRESENTATIVES,
COMMITTEE ON ENERGY AND COMMERCE,
SUBCOMMITTEE ON COMMERCE, CONSUMER PROTECTION,
AND COMPETITIVENESS,
*Washington, DC.*

The subcommittee met, pursuant to notice, at 10 a.m., in room 2322, Rayburn House Office Building, Hon. Cardiss Collins (chairwoman) presiding.

Mrs. COLLINS. Good morning. This hearing of the Energy and Commerce Subcommittee on Commerce, Consumer Protection and Competitiveness will come to order.

Consumers in today's global marketplace find it more and more difficult to determine the origin of products they buy. In the past, most consumers generally have believed that a product labeled "Made in America" was actually made here, including its components. Today, many products that are manufactured and assembled here contain components and materials that have come from many different countries.

Conversely, products that are assembled abroad may contain many components made here in the United States. The confusing question purchasers must try to answer is: What does "American Made" really mean nowadays? Consumers could get help in answering this difficult question if the bill we are considering today, H.R. 3342, were enacted.

This measure would require the Commerce Department to establish a toll-free number that consumers could call to get information about products that are made in America. Currently, no agency of the government collects this data and makes it available to consumers.

Under the bill, manufacturers could register products that are made in America with the Commerce Department. And in response to inquiries, the Commerce Department would then provide information to consumers regarding those which are listed and registered as being American-made.

If the manufacturer were to list a product with the Commerce Department that is not made in America, that manufacturer would not be able to offer the product for purchase by the Federal Government and would be subject to prosecution under section 5 of the Federal Trade Commission Act for making a deceptive claim. For purposes of this bill, "Made in America" is defined as: A product manufactured in the United States that contains components whose value exceeds 50 percent of the cost of all components used.

One of the important issues that this hearing will address is whether the definition is appropriate. This bill has a large number of cosponsors, which I believe reflects members' concerns that information concerning American-made products now available to consumers is simply inadequate.

We look forward to hearing from our witnesses as to how this bill may be used to give consumers the information they want and need.

[The text of H.R. 3342 follows:]

I

103D CONGRESS
1ST SESSION

# H. R. 3342

To establish a toll free number in the Department of Commerce to assist consumers in determining if products are American-made.

IN THE HOUSE OF REPRESENTATIVES

OCTOBER 21, 1993

Mr. TRAFICANT introduced the following bill; which was referred to the Committee on Energy and Commerce

# A BILL

To establish a toll free number in the Department of Commerce to assist consumers in determining if products are American-made.

*Be it enacted by the Senate and House of Representatives of the United States of America in Congress assembled,*

**SECTION 1. ESTABLISHMENT OF TOLL FREE NUMBER.**

(a) ESTABLISHMENT.—Within 180 days of the date of the enactment of this Act, the Secretary of Commerce shall establish a toll free number which may be used by consumers—

(1) to determine if a product is made in America, and

(2) learn where products may be purchased or learn a telephone number which will provide information on the purchase of products.

The Secretary shall publish the number in the Federal Register and undertake such outreach activities as may be appropriate to publicize the number.

(b) USE.—Consumers who use the toll free number shall be informed that the product list is not complete but is derived from registrations under section 2.

**SEC. 2. REGISTRATION.**

The Secretary of Commerce shall establish a procedure under which the manufacturer of a product which is made in America may register with the Secretary and have such product included in the information available through the toll free number established under section 1.

**SEC. 3. PENALTY.**

Any manufacturer of a product who registers a product with the Secretary of Commerce under section 2 which is not made in America may not offer such product for purchase by the Federal Government and shall be subject to prosecution under section 5 of the Federal Trade Commission Act for making a deceptive claim.

**SEC. 4. DEFINITION.**

For purposes of this Act, the term "made in America" means—

(1) an unmanufactured end product mined or produced in the United States, or

(2) an end product manufactured in the United States if the cost of its components mined, produced, or manufactured in the United States exceeds 50 percent of the cost of all of its components.

○

Mrs. COLLINS. Our ranking member and other members of the subcommittee are on their way, but at this time, we are going to recognize our witnesses because they are already here.

Our first witness is Hon. James A. Traficant Jr., of Ohio who is the author of the bill, our colleague, with whom we have worked for a very long period of time and who has been doing a lot of legislation, positive legislation about "Buy American" for a very long period of time.

We are glad to have you with us today, Mr. Traficant.

## STATEMENT OF HON. JAMES A. TRAFICANT, JR., A REPRESENTATIVE IN CONGRESS FROM THE STATE OF OHIO

Mr. TRAFICANT. I thank you, Chairwoman Collins.

I would like to submit first for the record a recommended amendment to my bill in the nature of a substitute that, in fact, would be a funding mechanism on how the 1-800 toll-free service would be paid for and financed.

Second of all, I would like to place in the record by unanimous consent, a letter I sent February 14th to the Department of Commerce. And I will read from paragraph 4 where I state that, "I would deeply appreciate any comments, suggestions or insights your office might have relative to H.R. 3342. Should the bill be approved by Congress, I stand ready to work with you and your staff to implement this worthwhile initiative."—I might also add, they never gave me the courtesy of a call, nor did they write me a letter.

I am trying to determine in all honestly before I go on with the testimony, if this is truly the position of the Secretary of Commerce, Ron Brown, who I have great respect for, or to be quite honest, a bunch of bureaucrats who have taken a position on this issue that may not necessarily be exactly what the Secretary might perhaps fashion.

Just briefly, it seems we are at odds and the Commerce Department tells me we are opposing it, but it is not, quote unquote, "contentious opposition." Well, the quote, unquote "contentious opposition" has never been written and I don't know if it has been conveyed to you, and that bothers me. I am trying to figure out what their opposition is because if their opposition would have come to me early enough, I would have addressed that.

I am not here trying to impose undue tasks on an already overburdened Commerce Department that says that they need all their free time to make sure that our exports get every opportunity they can; when we have a growing, since Richard Nixon, $60 billion trade deficit with Japan, and now a $26 billion trade deficit with China, second only to Japan, and they keep talking about what they are doing for American exports.

Be advised that under NAFTA, most of the "Buy American" laws are basically finished. With the new GATT agreement, nearly all "Buy American" provisions, which has become a contentious matter for many Members of Congress, "Buy American" will be a thing of the past.

So what I have done is I have taken a look at it. If you are an American worker and you have a job and you produce a product, that product sells and you get a paycheck and you pay taxes and you raise your family—if more and more imports keep coming in, there are very few incentives to "Buy American", there is not even a suggestion or recommendation to "Buy American."

I have lost 55,000 jobs in my district that average $14 an hour, Madam Chairwoman, with full benefits. They have been replaced with about 12,000 jobs that average $5 an hour with no benefits.

So, frankly, I am very upset with the position of the Commerce Department not giving me the courtesy of a call or drafting me a letter, because maybe I am not some big chairman. I am hot about it. I tell you right out.

Now, here is what my bill would do: My bill doesn't tell anybody what to buy, where to buy it or who to buy it from. It establishes, with absolute expediency, easily modified and codified in existing electronic technology available to the Congress, a 1-800 phone number that shall be advertised. And when a family wants to buy, for example, a refrigerator for their children getting married, they could call that number and say, look, I live in the State of Illinois, Chicago, and I want to know what refrigerators are made in America.

And, yes, the Commerce Department is going to have to say, sir—however they want to say it—this does not necessarily mean that there aren't other refrigerators made in America, but here is what we have on our list. The Westinghouse GT-26, the whatever product that we make, Philco brand, these are "Made in America" products that have been registered as made in America.

That doesn't mean that other products are not made in America. They simply may not be registered. And maybe that family would then say, I am going to shop for the Westinghouse or the Philco brands and compare them competitively.

Now, what the Commerce Department's position is saying is, look, we have very strict standards, Traficant. In order to put that label "Made in America", it has got to be made in America with 100 percent parts content.

Now, with all the debate we have had on the House Floor recently passing an amendment to the crime bill, which Commerce opposes, that would put a penalty on for a fraudulent label, I want to know what is 100 percent "Made in America", number one. I want to know the last time there was an investigation into a "Made in America" label that, in fact, assured 100 percent content.

And number three, if that is their real concern, you want to change the standard to "Made in America" to 100 percent, change it in a heartbeat. But if we are going to have a standard that says a "Made in America" label must be 100 percent made in America and the end product assembled in this country, so be it. But I want some enforcement of that, because here is what we are dealing with, Madam Chairwoman.

We are having products made in China at 17 cents an hour coming to this country, many times have fraudulent labels on them and our constituents think it is made by workers down the street to boot. I am absolutely, absolutely upset with the position of the Department not giving the courtesy of a call or a letter.

Now, specifically what this provides is a choice. The substitute provides for a funding mechanism. Here is how it would work.

The companies who want their product listed and registered would pay a fee. That fee would be established by the Department of Commerce. The Department of Commerce, according to the bill, shall, in fact, be compensated for their actual delivery of this system, the cost of the system. So there is not a cost to the Department of Commerce. And if, in fact, the program is developed pragmatically with some common sense, those true manufacturers of "Made in America" products will want to have their product listed.

Now, they can stratify those corporations which have a multitude of products that might be so listed, but no one is going to go down the street and ask what quilt is made in America or what smaller products might be made in America. More than likely, those companies who make ticket items which develop choice on a national agenda would probably want to have this additional "Made in America" known to the consumer.

I believe that it is becoming fashionable for American people to say, look, I would like to buy a "Made in America" product and I would like to know, and my God, if I could find out what refrigerator is made, I want to know. I want to know where the Buick Regal is made. I like the Regal. I want to know where the Camaro convertible is made. I want to know where the Ford pickup truck is made.

Right now, unless you read the VIN number or some fancy commercials that the companies advertise, does a company advertising an American-made product say this product is "Made in America" with 100 percent content?

The Traficant bill says the end product assembled in the country, at least 50 percent of its content is domestically produced. That is open. If this committee, subcommittee, would want to hold it to a higher standard, 100 percent "Made in America", I would advise this subcommittee to put some other language in there saying that there shall be a mechanism to enforce it. Because how many times do you go see a suit of clothes that said, "Made in America" with imported fabric.

I think a good question for this group is: What is "Made in America" with imported fabric and how the hell are they able to put a "Made in America" label in that coat?

Or the lawn mower that says "Made in America" with a foreign engine. The motor is 95 percent of the lawn mower, but it has a "Made in America" and then a small little tag that I will present to this committee—leave it open—as an example—and I want to incorporate it into the minutes—that says "Made in America" with an imported engine. The engine is 95 percent of a lawn mower. This is absolutely to me unbelievable.

There is no part of this bill that isn't flexible enough that you can put your fingerprints on it and change it. Here is what Jim Traficant is recommending to the Congress, that we do, in fact, have a hotline and when some consumer is going to make a ticket purchase price of some goods or service, they need within the definition of this bill, they can call and say, look, what is "Made in America?"

And yes, the Department of Commerce is going to have to assume a task. They are going to have to have somebody that, in fact, makes this response in a timely manner. There is going to be a charge to go ahead and effect that service, and that charge is, in fact, handled under the substitute whereby a registration fee for the companies who list their products shall be charged.

I know the concern is: Is this a "stamp of approval" by Uncle Sam? No, it is not. I mean, if companies can have small print that says "Made in America" with a foreign engine on a lawn mower, the Department of Commerce could say, these are registered products only. There could be other registered products made in America.

Quite frankly, I don't think that their arguments wash here, and here is where we are. We can't incentivize "Buy America." We can't give a weighted advantage.

I want you to imagine you are a steel company in Chicago or Youngstown, Ohio, and the Department of Transportation or the State of Ohio is buying thousands of tons of steel, thousands of tons of steel and a Chinese corporation is bidding on the steel; an American corporation is bidding on the steel and the average labor factor in the steel-making apparatus in our country is minimal, $20 an hour, minimum.

That Chinese steel is made at 17 cents an hour. With the Most Favored Nation trade status, they send it over basically uninterrupted. We can't even offer an incentive to purchase the American-made steel.

Now, we have opened up a massive trade agreement with Mexico and Canada, and before I close off—and good to see the members coming in—that company that operates in Chicago or operates in Youngstown or operates in Newark has a deal with IRS and social security, workmen's comp, unemployment comp, banking regulations, security regulations, OSHA, EPA, labor laws, minimum wage, pay an average manufacturing cost of $25 an hour.

Right now, American law says that same company I just talked about can move to Mexico tomorrow, no IRS, no social security, no workmen's comp, no unemployment comp, no OSHA, no EPA, no banking regulation, no social security regulation. Our people bid at a dollar an hour. Anybody that says that it takes five Mexicans to do the job of one American is making a racist statement. Mexican workers are hungry to work, they're well trained, they do just as good a job as the American worker.

So here we are now. We open up the doors. You are in business. You can get all these shackles off your back, go right across the border, step on the other side of this table, you are in Mexico, send us your product. We can't even tell you the requirements of that truck driver because they don't fall under, don't need a driver's license. There isn't even a human rights condition on that contract. So what is left?

I am saying, the least that we could do is tell some American who wants to buy an American-made product what is made in America. And the United States Commerce Department is technically finding fault with it; didn't respond to me since February the 14th—and, Congressman, we want to see more products purchased in America, maybe we could sit down and find some common ground—don't call me back. Then before this meeting, give me a bunch of garbage here. But then one assistant says: But we are really not contentious in our opposition, Congressman—that is what is wrong with the damn country.

I do have 234 cosponsors. They don't understand the position taken by the Department of Commerce. The Department of Commerce is hoping they can get to those members and screw it around.

But just two quick points. Several quick points and then I will leave you to your deliberations: On the 1-800 service, because there has been also some talk about pragmatics, process, the Commerce Department wouldn't need to procure special equipment to set up this toll-free number—I want this on the record—because the FTS-2000 system is compatible with switched-voice service, number one.

The bottom line is the 1-800 number could easily be installed on Commerce's existing FTS-2000 phone system. Under the FTS-2000 system, AT&T could provide Commerce with usage-sensitive pricing based on the time of day, distance and volume. This will save Commerce significant dollars in operating costs once the 1-800 number is up and running, and allowing Commerce to set a reasonable registration fee.

The setting of the fee is in their hands. The FTS-2000 system is versatile enough to allow Commerce to do a number of things with the 1-800 number, such as sophisticated routing, as well as management information reports that will let Commerce know how the 1-800 number is being used and how it is in fact being engaged.

Other available features the AT&T and the FTS system will offer that will help Commerce, contrary to what has been bandied around, include the following:

Time of day call routing. This feature allows the change of routing of calls automatically, depending on the time of day.

Second, is day of the week routing. The feature allows that they can route calls to different offices or personnel depending on the day of the week.

Third, is call distribution routing. The feature allocates calls to different offices on a percentage basis to balance work loads and redistribute calls to keep operations running smoothly.

Number four, command routing. The feature allows the diversion of calls to other offices or locations on holidays or emergencies, such as snow days or other days that would ensure the callers get service.

The overall cost of setting up a 1-800 service is very reasonable and most flexible. There is no other cost-effective way of trying to incentivize under current law, with GATT coming down the pike, a methodology by which Americans can understand what is available for procurement that is truly American.

If Commerce does a good job of publicizing the program, which the bill says they shall publicize this phone number and this service, I anticipate that a large number of American companies will participate because they will not only take pride in the fact that it is "Made in America", they realize they are at times facing opposition from very cheap import products, and the American people will give them an edge.

With the imposition of a modest registration fee, Commerce can then be able to fund the program without one additional penny of budgeted moneys from this Congress and it is very simple. If I was taking the gaff in America, making the product, investing in our country, hiring American people, facing all these regulations and the high production costs we have, I would want the American people to know that product is made in America.

Now, the 100-percent standard that they talk about, they are against this bill. That is a smoke screen, because I think it is almost unenforceable and I want to know the last time they enforced one of these. My information tells me that it was 20 years ago where they had a case such as this. But if "Made in America" is completely open in this bill, Madam Chairwoman, if that is their contention and it has got to be 100-percent "Made in America", so be it.

But the Traficant bill says: Assembled in this country and 50 percent of its parts and contents domestically produced. Now, you are going to say, well, how are we going to enforce that, Congressman? Well, just remember this. An automobile, if that engine is made in America, would solve it right now, and it is not as tough as we think for Commerce to set up some system.

But where does the burden lie under the bill? The burden lies with the company and if that company lies or submits information that is not, in fact—any manufacturer of product who registers such product with the Secretary of Commerce under section 2 which is not "Made in America" according to the definition would then not be able to offer such product for purchase by the Federal Government and shall be subject to prosecution under existing law.

I think times have changed and I think a 50-percent standard is fine enough with me, but if they want to make it 100-percent standard, fine, I have no problem with that. I just want to see the initiation of the service. I think it would give the American people an opportunity to select an American-made product.

And that is my statement and I would ask unanimous consent that all of my pieces of information here be incorporated into the minutes of this meeting, and I thank the chairwoman.

[The letter previously referred to follows:]

JAMES A. TRAFICANT, JR.
17TH DISTRICT, OHIO

COMMITTEES
COMMITTEE ON PUBLIC WORKS AND TRANSPORTATION
CHAIRMAN, SUBCOMMITTEE ON PUBLIC BUILDINGS AND GROUNDS
SUBCOMMITTEE ON ECONOMIC DEVELOPMENT
SUBCOMMITTEE ON SURFACE TRANSPORTATION
COMMITTEE ON SCIENCE, SPACE, AND TECHNOLOGY
SUBCOMMITTEE ON SPACE
SELECT COMMITTEE ON NARCOTICS ABUSE AND CONTROL

**Congress of the United States**
**House of Representatives**
**Washington, DC 20515–3517**

2446 RAYBURN HOUSE OFFICE BUILDING
WASHINGTON, DC 20515
(202) 225-5261

11 OVERHILL ROAD
YOUNGSTOWN, OH 44512
(216) 788-2414

5555 YOUNGSTOWN-WARREN ROAD
SUITE 2685
NILES, OH 44446
(216) 652-5649

109 WEST 3RD STREET
EAST LIVERPOOL, OH 43920
(216) 385-5921

February 14, 1994

The Honorable Ronald H. Brown
Secretary
U. S. Department of Commerce
14th Street and Constitution Avenue, N.W.
Washington, D.C. 20230

Dear Secretary Brown:

I am writing in regards to legislation I introduced last fall, H.R. 3342, to establish a toll-free phone number that consumers could call to get information on products made in America. For your easy reference, I have attached a copy of the bill, which has 232 co-sponsors.

If they had a choice, most Americans would want to buy American-made goods. A toll-free number is an excellent way to promote the "Made in the USA" theme. H.R. 3342, would direct the U.S. Department of Commerce to establish the toll-free number. The bill also directs the Commerce Department to publicize the number and to develop a registration system for American companies to have their products included in the program. The bill would subject any companies providing false information to federal penalties. The bill also requires that consumers calling the number be informed that the list of American-made goods is not a complete list. As I noted above, the program would be self-funding through a registration fee.

H.R. 3342 represents a small, but important step, towards preserving and expanding American manufacturing. Best of all, it won't cost the taxpayers a dime.

I would deeply appreciate any comments, suggestions or insights your office might have relative to H.R. 3342. Should the bill be approved by Congress, I stand ready to work with you and your staff to implement this worthwhile initiative.

Thank you in advance for your time and consideration. I look forward to your response.

Respectfully,

James A. Traficant, Jr.
Member of Congress

JAT/pm

Attachment

Mrs. COLLINS. The time of the gentleman has expired.

Without objection, the addenda to your statement, your written statement will be made a part of the record, as will your entire statement be made part of the record.

Mr. Traficant, there are probably millions of different products to which this bill could apply, and my question is whether it is your intention that the Commerce Department investigates each product that a manufacturer claims to be American-made to determine whether the manufacturer's representation is valid?

Mr. TRAFICANT. The bill does not call for the Department of Commerce to investigate each claim. In fact, to the contrary. Listen to what the bill says: American manufacturers, tell us truthfully because we are going to accept your word, but if there is a complaint that comes in here and you are telling us that model 126 lawn mower is really made in China, then we are going to investigate it and if we find out that lawn mower is really made in China, you cannot sell any of your products to Uncle Sam. You are barred from procurement with the Federal Government and, in fact, you are subject to prosecution.

The burden in the Traficant bill is not on the Commerce Department. Yes, the Commerce Department is eventually going to have to find out and really get a grip on what is made in America, and it is evident; I wonder how much of a grip they have now, Madam Chairwoman.

So, again, there is not a burden on them under this bill regardless of how they interpret or imagine this bill to apply. And if, in fact, there are some nebulous areas that could lead in that direction, I welcome the input of the committee to clarify it with additional supportive language.

Mrs. COLLINS. So with the burden not being on the Commerce Department, obviously there are some penalties that would be involved. The burden then would rests with the manufacturer for giving an incorrect statement?

Mr. TRAFICANT. For giving an incorrect statement.

However, I would assume that once the Commerce Department—let's say the Commerce Department is not able to defeat this initiative and it would become law. The Commerce Department, within a wide range of their activities, could very easily set up a regulatory process to do at least some scope looking at these products.

For example, I am a company. I say, my lawn mower is made in America. In fact, all of it is made in America here and I want it registered. Sure, the Commerce Department probably sent back a form letter: Answer the following questions.

They might go ahead and do something like that. My bill doesn't prohibit them from doing something like that. If they wanted to go investigate these cases, they could. But what the Traficant bill says right now is the burden is on the manufacturer, and if, in fact, you are not telling the truth and if it does become investigated, the Commerce Department then, in taking action, you are prohibited from selling to Uncle Sam, the big procurer, number one; and number two, you can be, in fact, subject to prosecution under existing law.

But isn't that where we are now? We are putting a "Made in America" on there now. How do we deal with it now when someone is saying it is "Made in America", but it is not. When is the last time we really did something on that?

Mrs. COLLINS. Do you have any idea what kind of staff resources the Commerce Department might have to have to devote to the implementation of your bill?

Mr. TRAFICANT. I do not know, Madam Chairwoman, but here is what I do know. It is self-funding. Maybe it will create a few jobs.

Mrs. COLLINS. It might be self-funding, but wouldn't that drain some of the resources that they have to take care of other activities that they are already doing?

Are you saying the funding would be enough to add new employees if they needed them?

Mr. TRAFICANT. They right now don't have this service and they don't do it. Whatever they do, they would have to get the funds to do it. And the funds would come through the self-funding mechanism of the Traficant substitute that says the fee shall be charged with a company registers its product. They would have to promulgate and say what is it going to cost us to run this thing, all right, here is the fee structure we are going to set up. And they would hire some people. They would hire some people, Americans, for a system like this.

Mrs. COLLINS. In order to be listed on the list that you are proposing, manufacturers would have to pay a fee to the Commerce Department, where is the incentive for them to do so?

Mr. TRAFICANT. They don't need to do so. The incentive is that once that number becomes public, those companies that realize that they are in a competitive marketplace with products that are made many times overseas, those products overseas cannot be listed and it is a competitive advantage for them to list their product under a "Made in America" hotline.

Mrs. COLLINS. Now, you mentioned NAFTA. In the NAFTA agreement, a product has to be 60 percent American, Mexican or Canadian contents in order to be considered a North American product.

For purposes of determining CAFE, only those vehicles with 75 percent United States content can be considered domestic U.S. and the Federal Trade Commission has required that to avoid a charge of making a deceptive claim, that a product is made in America, 100-percent product would have to be made here in America.

Now, in your bill, products with 50 percent or more U.S. content would be considered American made. How do you come up with the 50-percent number; and might 50 percent be too low in light of these higher requirements under other laws?

Mr. TRAFICANT. It is open if you want to change it, but here is what the Traficant bill says that: Buick Regal that is assembled in Canada could not be listed under the Traficant bill as "Made in America."

It is not "Made in America" under the Traficant bill. I don't care how much content it has. It is assembled in Canada with Canadian workers.

The Traficant bill says the end product, the end product manufactured is American. That is the assembly. So that Cavalier made in Youngstown, Ohio is an American product. That Saturn made in Tennessee would become an American product. But that truck,

Ford truck, Chevy truck, Chevy Camaro, Pontiac Firebird made in Canada is not an American made under the Traficant bill.

Traficant doesn't say North American, it says American. Our 50 States. So that pineapple, for example, crazy as it sounds, Dole says—Dole is known for pineapple. Most of the pineapple—check with Patsy Mink—the Dole pineapple now is coming from the Philippines.

Everybody thinks they are buying American, Hawaiian pineapple. I don't mean to get into those types of abstract settings, but under the Traficant bill, assembled in our 50 States and the domestic contents, at least 50 percent of them are produced in America.

I can go higher, but the truth of the matter is I would rather have an assembly provision rather than a 75 or 100 percent North American business. My people can't move to Canada to get a job. But you see, under an item like this, if there is a car that might be popular, they have to say: We have a popular car here, people are calling and saying, "Why don't you make that car in America?"

Maybe, just maybe, Buick might bring that Regal plant to your district or mine or an assembly, part of it, maybe not all of it, but the point is you buy a Buick Regal, you are buying a car made by Canadian hands, and many of these other cars you make are now being made in Mexico. If that car doesn't have a number 1 on the VIN number, it is not made in our proper 50 States; number 2, Canada; number 3, Mexico, Japan, J; Korean, K. I mean, most Americans don't even know when they see a Buick, Buick Regal is made in Canada, Madam Chairwoman.

Here is what I am saying. This is open for you to tailor, but under the Traficant bill, that car to be American made must be assembled in this country with at least 50 percent of its parts and contents domestically produced.

Mrs. COLLINS. Mr. Stearns.

Mr. STEARNS. Madam Chairwoman, thank you very much.

My good friend, Mr. Traficant, good morning and we welcome you to the committee. I think your bill is very symbolic and it is—as you know, it is a bill that I support in concept.

In looking through or talking with staff about it, would you be willing to work with members of this subcommittee, both sides of the aisle to, refine some of the language in the fee section so it will not require any budget waivers when this bill goes to the Floor?

Mr. TRAFICANT. Absolutely.

Mr. STEARNS. OK.

Mr. TRAFICANT. Any part of this bill—not to interrupt you, Mr. Stearns—any part of this bill is open for improvement by your subcommittee. It is my idea and the firm commitment to those products that I bring this bill forward.

Mr. STEARNS. Good. Good.

The chairwoman had discussed this 50 percent threshold that you have in your bill. You know, I followed the crime bill and you contained a threshold of 60 percent. You had there an FTC case law on the subject requires 100 percent domestic content—and I think she has already asked how you came up with the 50 percent. It sounds like you are flexible on that, too.

Mr. TRAFICANT. I am, but the reason why I have done that is because this content business is so convoluted in some areas. My bill says American hands must assemble it in or on the earth of our 50 States, and I have left a lesser—a lesser area because there are many components to some of these specific things and I wanted to make sure that basically a large percentage, at least half, is American made.

So the standards they have look great. Everybody brags about these great standards, but the truth of the matter is, Mr. Stearns, those great standards, in my opinion, are never really enforced, nor do they even investigate it.

Mr. STEARNS. There are a lot of positive symbolic ideas that you have in this bill. The thing I guess I am concerned with is the enforcement of this bill and what kind of enforcement, I guess, through the FTC and others, will we be adding a whole dimension of regulation. And, you know, prosecution which will be more or less just more of this regulation that you talk about in your 1 minute every day, the increased government regulations and the—you know, so I think both you and I share about, are we going to put a bill in that is going to add a new dimension of regulation of Federal enforcement?

A lot of bills you mentioned—that is why people are leaving the United States to go to Mexico. Now you are proposing a bill that essentially is perhaps adding more regulation.

Mr. TRAFICANT. All of the statutes that deal with fraudulent labels and all those different things are already on the book. I think what you are now talking about I think is a very good analogy here is, not necessarily whether or not that prosecutorial element is there or law is there to effect such regulation, but it is never being used, and, yes, under this bill, there may be some of these doldrums of unused enforcement that might become used. I will admit to that. But the point is, again, "Made in America" with imported fabric.

Mr. STEARNS. What are you going to do about Samoa and Guam and some of the territories?

Mr. TRAFICANT. I think our bill, they would be covered by the bill or I would be welcoming a provision for it.

Mr. STEARNS. So those territories you would consider part of the United States?

Mr. TRAFICANT. It would be open for your interpretation. I would leave that open for you if that would be a problem.

Mr. STEARNS. I am going to give a hypothetical to follow your idea.

Mr. TRAFICANT. Don't make it too tough.

Mr. STEARNS. We got a pretty tough one here. Let me read it to you. This goes into my idea of increasing the regulations.

Let's look at hypothetical situation of a computer manufacturer in the United States that contains 51 percent domestic content, according to the definition in your bill, and they register their product with the Commerce Department. Say, that they buy certain chips from a manufacturing facility in California and those chips comprise 2 percent of the cost of the computer. When the California facility shuts down due to a strike for a month, the computer company is forced to cover with chips from Asia, reducing their domestic content to 49 percent for that month. Assuming that the product is registered with the Department of Commerce, would the Federal

Trade Commission be able to bring an action against the company for having a deceptive claim if it continues to ship computers during that month?

Mr. TRAFICANT. Let's just think about it. If we are going to split hairs on such technicalities, and I agree that we have to look at that—here is the Department of Commerce. The Department of Commerce knows that a company has had a strike and that strike now has forced them to use some foreign chips, which may, in fact, bring their total domestic requirement under the bill's threshold.

I think if you want to put a provision there saying: For such activities, that such abstract phenomena would not be subject to enforcement, I think it would just be common sense, and the Department of Commerce is not going to jump on somebody who has a strike trying to stay afloat and language could be in to protect that.

Mr. STEARNS. But we could assume instead after 2 percent of the chip—the chip represents 2 percent, it could be 10 percent.

Mr. TRAFICANT. Frightening.

Mr. STEARNS. The strike instead of a month could be 6 months and all this would be thrown into the mix.

Mr. TRAFICANT. I think in such a situation though, that if it would require some specific language, I think that could be developed in the basic regulations, though, once the Department of Commerce notifies these companies. There are going to be situations that may produce some variables.

I think that is why the 50 percent threshold, first of all, is much more practicable than this so-called 100 percent. But they could use or you could set a standard of maybe a yearly average or production life run of a particular piece of equipment, Model-T-1000 computer and on the life run of it, that they are maintaining on their life run, that they are showing an average of 50 percent, that average could be put in.

These are things that I am not so sure we have to do here. I think that if the Department of Commerce got this charge, the Department of Commerce could basically stratify this pretty easily. They could set up a fee schedule. The companies will pay for it. If companies don't want to pay to have their products listed, they don't have to. But if they are making a product that "Made in America" qualifies, and their competitor is having that product registered, they will be behooved competitively to get that product out there. Because that lets the American people know, look, ours is made here, ours is registered, American workers get a paycheck to help run this thing. It could become a part of their marketing tool. That is what will happen to these companies who will say, look, what advantage do I have. My God, let me take a good stroke here and get the American people on our side. And I see that happening, Mr. Stearns.

Mr. STEARNS. Thank you, Madam Chairwoman.

Mrs. COLLINS. Mr. Greenwood.

Mr. GREENWOOD. Thank you, Madam Chairwoman.

Good morning.

Mr. TRAFICANT. Good morning.

Mr. GREENWOOD. I share your goal. I hope that your bill can be worked out so that it can become law and it can work. I have a big question in my mind about whether it can. Let me ask you some questions to help me decide.

First off, clearly your intention is that we would have a fee paid by the manufacturers that would cover the costs incurred by Commerce for their personnel, et cetera to implement this program. I can understand how you could argue that is not an expansion of the budget, nor is it a take down on the resources of Commerce, because we are going to pay for new personnel and new resources from these fees.

How does this proposal interface with the Vice President's goal of reducing the Federal work force by several 252,000? The Congress and the administration are committed to a net reduction in the Federal work force. I believe this is a proposal that will require a lot of personnel to administer.

Mr. TRAFICANT. First of all, I don't think it is going to require as much personnel as everybody is saying it is.

Second of all, it is self-funding, and third of all, the Traficant bill doesn't even say the Commerce Department has to do it. It says the Commerce Department has to do it, but the Commerce Department I believe, or they could even contract this service out.

Now, I wouldn't support that, but if we are really worried about funds, what is the general net impact of revenue from products made in America that keeps American workers working. So when you look at the other side of this, you see there is a revenue source that comes into this government by people who are working and pay taxes. People who work building things in our country. If they don't build things, they don't pay taxes.

So we are going to have dependent citizens or self-actualized independent citizens who are workers and contribute. So my bill says, yes, they will offset it with a fee and that fee will cover all of their expenses.

This has nothing to do with Vice President's Al Gore's position on staffing. It is not a part of the equation right now, and if there is, in fact, staffing for it, it would have to be created and financed through this self-funding mechanism.

Mr. GREENWOOD. If——

Mr. TRAFICANT. Much of this would be technological, I might add, Mr. Greenwood, believe me, and it would be pretty hard for me to answer that specifically. But it is not my goal to saddle another bureaucratic administration, that is what they are trying to maintain, but there is no other real highlights of American-made products.

Mr. GREENWOOD. I understand what you are saying. If this is going to be funded with private dollars, and if you say it theoretically could be staffed with contracted private sector employees, then I am led to believe that the whole ball of wax could be done privately.

In other words, there is nothing to prevent American manufacturers who think they could gain a competitive advantage by having this toll-free number, from setting up such an operation, paying for it and staffing it.

Mr. TRAFICANT. But the problem is we haven't seen anything to that effect at this point. If we are going to incentivize the purchase of American-made products, that is probably a responsibility the Congress should undertake. The contracting out would fly in the face of my philosophy on this issue. But again, much of the issuing and the delivery of this service here is technology, and with the FTS system that AT&T currently has, much of this can be coordinated through such a sophisticated 800-service number.

So I think what we are looking at is this bill and the concept of this bill would carry along the stamp of the United States Government, there is no doubt about it. And the Department of Commerce, in acting on behalf of the Congress of the United States is saying, look, we can't stop anybody from selling their product here. We can't stop anything happening with Mexico and Canada under the law. Under GATT there is no "Buy American" law, but here is what the Congress is saying: We officially, our government, want to let the people of America know what is made in America and we are providing an opportunity for companies who take pride to be involved in the program.

Mr. GREENWOOD. I understand the concept.

The other question I have is this. I think you are absolutely right that having your product listed as you would like it to be listed under this proposal would create a competitive advantage for a manufacturer. It therefore also leads me to believe that disadvantaged companies may want to challenge the listing of a product. If my product is only 45 percent made in America and my competitor figures out how to make it at 55 percent so he is eligible for your list, I may want to call the Department of Commerce and challenge my competitor's product listing. I would want you to do an investigation.

Is it your view that Commerce would have to investigate every complaint made by a competitor?

Mr. TRAFICANT. I doubt it, and there could be regs that could be worked out through the subcommittee or through them that would say it would have to be a FTC process or an official action taken. Somebody can't just call the hotline and say John Doe did something, investigate him. I think it is important, there now, for the first time, would be a mechanism where a company that feels they are being really hurt by an imported product that is falsely coming forward, would have an opportunity for some redress.

Let me briefly, I don't want to take up too much more time of this subcommittee. Let me tell you this. I got involved in a case in Cincinnati and nearby northern Kentucky over a company called Mazak, Incorporated. Mazak, think about it. They had a contract with a couple of other air bases, government contract.

It was a young Marine that worked for them and finally reported that had they had a "Buy American" provision and certain items were coming from Japan that were imports and then they were taking those imports and putting a fraudulent label on them and used them in other ports of call. Our Commerce Department didn't even investigate it.

In all fairness to Ron Brown, Ron Brown was not the Secretary. I got involved in the case, and a year later got 60 Minutes to investigate it. Mazak was a wholly-owned subsidiary of Yamasaki, Inc., the largest manufacturer of tool and other products, and they just simply did not buy it from their company in Florence, Kentucky. They were stone cold imports. And they got hit and it took 60 Minutes to hit them. Go to Cincinnati.

Now, under the Traficant 1-800, here is a company that said they produce a product. Here is a good way for a company to say we know ours is made in America; you show us yours is made in America.

How do we stop this? Where is the enforcement? It takes 60 Minutes to investigate Mazak, Incorporated, of Kentucky in the Cincinnati area, and Channel 9 of Cincinnati to bring it to the attention of—joint efforts with 60 Minutes, CBS, to get an investigation. Read that case file.

So the point I am making is, look, there are a lot of areas where you could take a shot at this thing. Here is what I am upset about today, we are opposed to it, but it is not "contentious opposition." What is that?

Second of all, February 14th, I sent a letter, I says: Tell me whatever you can do to improve this. I never got a call back. I was told that they didn't have "contentious opposition." Hell, they are going to get more than contentious opposition from me and I want the help of the subcommittee.

Make it better, handle your concerns, but let's at least let an American know what is made in the country. We can't do anything else.

Mrs. COLLINS. The time of Mr. Greenwood has expired.

We thank you, Mr. Traficant, for presenting your bill before the subcommittee today.

Thank you very much.

Mr. TRAFICANT. Thank you, Madam Chairwoman.

Thank you, members.

Mrs. COLLINS. Our next witness is T.S. Chung, Director from the Office of Export Promotion, Department of Commerce.

Won't you come forward please, Mr. Chung.

You may begin your testimony at this time.

## STATEMENT OF T.S. CHUNG, DIRECTOR, OFFICE OF EXPORT PROMOTION, DEPARTMENT OF COMMERCE

Mr. CHUNG. Good morning, Madam Chairwoman and members of the subcommittee. My name is Chung, and I am the Director of the Office of Export Promotion Coordination, Trade Development, which is within the International Trade Administration at the Department of Commerce.

I do appreciate the opportunity to appear before you today to discuss H.R. 3342. As you know, I have submitted a written statement and ask that it be made a part of the record.

Mrs. COLLINS. Without objection.

Mr. CHUNG. Thank you very much.

I am not—I have to tell you that I am not prepared to answer every question that Mr. Traficant has raised during the last hour, but I will go on with my remarks.

I do appreciate your and Congressman Traficant's comments this morning. We welcome Congressional interest in raising the awareness of American consumers to products made in the United States. We believe that they are among the best and most competitive in the world, deserving consideration by consumers in the United States and overseas. In fact, the principal business of the International Trade Administration is to promote and assist U.S.

industry to penetrate foreign markets and to increase its market share. My job as the Director of Office of Export Promotion is to coordinate many programs of the Department that promote exports of American goods and services.

With respect to labeling of products, however, the Department of Commerce has a very limited role. The Federal Government involvement in this area, as you are probably aware, is handled primarily by the Federal Trade Commission. In addition, the Treasury Department's U.S. Customs Service has sole responsibility for country-of-origin marking of imports.

I will provide the committee with a brief overview of the current "Made in America" labeling requirements administered by these two agencies, but would have to defer to them on the details of the current laws and practices and of the effect of this legislative proposal on their programs. I will then explain why the Department of Commerce has concerns regarding this bill.

Let me first talk to you briefly about the U.S. Customs Service. The U.S. Customs Service enforces country-of-origin markings, duty assessments and import quotas. Under section 304 of the Tariff Act of 1930, imported products generally must contain a label indicating country of origin.

Current law and enforcement practice, as we understand it, require that unless imported products undergo substantial transformation in the United States, they must bear a label stating the product's foreign country of origin. If the product does undergo substantial transformation, the manufacturer may then choose to label a product "Made in America" but the label must also disclose the source of any foreign components.

With certain exceptions, U.S. law does not require U.S.-made products to bear a label "Made in America", however, if such a label is used, it must be truthful, and that is where the FTC comes in. The FTC has the statutory responsibility for protecting U.S. consumers from deceptive practices, including assuring that labeling of products does not deceive U.S. consumers. The focus of FTC regulations and enforcement is that product labels be truthful and meet consumers' expectations of what is meant by "Made in America."

Under current practice, as we understand it, FTC allows products to be labeled as "Made in America" without qualifications, only if 100 percent of the product, that is parts and labor, is of U.S. origin.

As we understand it, FTC seems to believe that the consumers expect that a product with a "Made in America" label is made 100 percent in America. If less than 100 percent of the total finished in product is of U.S. origin and if the manufacturer wishes to use a "Made in America" label, the label must also disclose foreign source content of the product. That is how we have a label such as "Made in America" with Chinese parts.

These labeling and marking requirements enforced by the FTC and Customs ensure that U.S. customers, consumers have access to accurate country-of-origin information. Such information is probably one of several factors consumers take into account in making purchasing decisions. Both agencies will investigate and address complaints that a product is mislabeled or deceptive.

Now, let me tell you why the Department of Commerce has concerns regarding this bill. The proposed definition of "Made in America" in H.R. 3342 could actually weaken the standards contained in current practice and law as administered by the FTC.

Further, it is specifically contrary to the Textile Fiber Products Identification Act and the Wool Products Labeling Act of 1939. If enacted, H.R. 3342 would not require the disclosure of the foreign component parts of a product. Current law and practice is actually more helpful to consumers in this regard.

Application of "Made in America" rule to exports could conflict with the importing country's country-of-origin marking requirements. For instance, a U.S. manufacturer of goods that qualify as U.S. goods under the rules-of-origin in a foreign market but that do not qualify for the "Made in America" labeling under this proposal could actually lose the potential business benefit of such a label advertising the American quality of the exported product.

If I may have just one additional minute?

Mrs. COLLINS. Of course.

Mr. CHUNG. Thank you.

There are already several private sector initiatives to bring "Made in America" information to the attention of consumers as best they can. Examples of such initiatives are presented in my written statement.

As briefly alluded to, the program could be costly to administer in both dollar and resource allocation terms. The potential fee to cover all the costs of setting up, publicizing, running and continually updating the database could be prohibitive for manufacturers, especially for small businesses. It would also impose a heavy paperwork burden on the businesses to back up its claim of the products being made in America.

In addition, companies both large and small would be forced to set up elaborate recordkeeping to track the everchanging product composition. Alternatively, any registration fees would be passed on to the consumer, raising the price of the product. The end result could be that companies would forego using a "Made in America" label altogether, further limiting consumer information.

Finally, the legislation also raises a disturbing possibility that the program could be viewed as a U.S. Government stamp of approval.

In conclusion, for the reasons I have stated, we cannot support H.R. 3342. I realize that this is probably not what you wanted to hear, but we do appreciate your, as well as Congressman Traficant's continued and unwavering support for U.S.-made products.

Our work at the Department of Commerce to promote U.S. goods and services shares the same goal of ensuring a healthy, growing economy with good, high-paying jobs for Americans.

We look forward to working with you, Madam Chairwoman, and the other members of the committee to advance these goals.

I would be pleased to answer any questions that you may have.

[The prepared statement of Mr. Chung follows:]

TESTIMONY OF
T.S. CHUNG, DIRECTOR
OFFICE OF EXPORT PROMOTION COORDINATION
TRADE DEVELOPMENT, INTERNATIONAL TRADE ADMINISTRATION
U.S. DEPARTMENT OF COMMERCE
MAY 19, 1994

before

COMMITTEE ON ENERGY AND COMMERCE
SUBCOMMITTEE ON COMMERCE, CONSUMER PROTECTION
AND COMPETITIVENESS

Madam Chairwoman, Members of the Subcommittee, I appreciate the opportunity to appear before you today to discuss H.R. 3342.

We welcome Congressional interest in raising the awareness of the American consumer to products made in the United States. We know that many Americans would prefer to buy products made by American workers. To that end, the Administration is committed to strong enforcement of product labeling laws, including those relating to labeling of country of origin.

We strongly believe that products made in the United States are among the best and most competitive in the world and deserve consideration by consumers not only in the United States but throughout foreign markets. In fact, the principal business of the International Trade Administration is to promote U.S. products and services overseas and to assist U.S. industry to penetrate foreign markets and to increase its market share. As director of the Office of Export Promotion Coordination in the International Trade Administration, my job is to coordinate the many programs of the Department that promote exports of American goods and services.

However, I want to emphasize the Department of Commerce's very limited role in Made in America labeling issues. Federal government involvement in this area is handled primarily by the Federal Trade Commission (FTC), while the Treasury Department's U.S. Customs Service has sole responsibility for country of origin marking of imports. I will provide the Committee with a brief overview of current "Made in America" labeling requirements as administered by these two agencies but would defer to them on the details of current law and practice and of the effect of this legislative proposal on their programs.

The U.S. Customs Service of the Department of the Treasury enforces duty assessments and import quotas. Under Section 304 of the Tariff Act of 1930, imported products generally must contain a label indicating country of origin. Current law and enforcement practice, as we understand it, requires that unless imported products undergo substantial transformation in the United States they must bear a label stating the product's foreign country of origin. In addition, under Federal Trade

Commission practices, if the manufacturer chooses to label a product "Made in America," the product must not only undergo "substantial transformation" in the United States, but also be manufactured from 100 percent U.S. components or disclose the source of any foreign components.

The Federal Trade Commission has the statutory responsibility for protecting U.S. consumers from deceptive practices, including assuring that labeling of products does not act to deceive the U.S. consumer. The focus of FTC regulations and enforcement is that product labels meet consumers' expectations of what is meant by "Made in America".

With certain exceptions, U.S. law does not require U.S.-made products to bear a label "Made in America"; however, if such a label is used, it must be truthful. Under current practice, as we understand it, the Federal Trade Commission allows products to be labeled as "Made in America" without qualifications, only if 100 percent or substantially all of the product (parts and labor) is U.S. origin. If less than 100 percent of the total cost of the finished product is U.S. origin and if the manufacturer wishes to use a "Made in America" label, the label also must disclose foreign-source content of the product.

These labeling and marking requirements, enforced by the FTC and Customs, ensure that U.S. consumers have access to information to make purchasing decisions based on accurate country-of-origin information. Both agencies will investigate and address complaints that a product is mislabeled or deceptive.

We are concerned that, as currently drafted, H.R. 3342 could actually weaken the standards contained in current practice and law as administered by the FTC. Further, the proposed definition of "Made in America" in H.R. 3342 is specifically contrary to the Textile Fiber Products Identification Act (Textiles Fiber Act) and the Wool Products labeling Act of 1939 (Wool Products Act). For example, if enacted, H.R. 3342 would not require the disclosure of the foreign component parts of a product, as is currently required under the FTC administrative rules, the Textiles Fiber Act and the Wool Products Act. Accordingly, current law and practice is more helpful to the consumer in this regard, allowing them to make a fully informed purchasing decision.

The legislation is unclear as to whether these registration procedures and labeling requirements would apply to all U.S. products, including those destined for the export market. Application of the "Made in America" rule to exports could conflict with the importing country's country-of-origin marking requirements. For example, other countries may apply laws similar to Section 304 of the Tariff Act of 1930 which require that all imports conspicuously indicate their country of origin.

U.S. manufacturers of goods that qualify as U.S. goods under the rules of origin in a foreign market but that do not qualify for the "Made in America" labeling under this proposal, could also lose the potential business benefit of such a label advertising the American quality of the product.

In addition, the legislation also could cause confusion with country-of-origin determinations for tariff treatment in foreign markets. A product could qualify as U.S.-origin for foreign tariff purposes, yet not comply with the proposed "Made in America" rule.

The private sector has seen the desire of U.S. consumers to find and buy products made in America. There already are several private sector initiatives to bring such information to the attention of the consumer as best they can. Without endorsing any of the commercial publications, following are examples of such publications:

- Buy American: How to Handbook, Annette Donoho, Waikoloa, Hawaii, December 1991.

- Made in the U.S.A.: The Complete Guide to America's Finest Products, Made in the U.S.A. Foundation, National Press Books, Washington, D.C., 1992.

- A quarterly newsletter published by the non-profit Buy America Foundation, William J. Lynott, Abington, Pennsylvania 19001.

- Flag Labelling All Goods and Services (FLAGS) Foundation, Rapid City, South Dakota, which will give the Country of Ownership of the Company, Where the product is made, and Where parts are made.

- We are aware of at least one other publication due out in June or July of this year: Buyers Guide to American Products: From Automobiles to Video Programs, Citadel Press, Carol Publishing, New York.

The Department of Commerce is very concerned that a program such as that proposed in H.R. 3342 could be costly to administer in both dollar and resource allocation terms. The number of companies, multiplied by the number of products could be tremendous, especially considering that product lines and manufacturing processes change frequently in this global economy. In order to provide consumers with useful information and reasonable choices, the register would have to contain a tremendous number of listings. There is also a question of how often manufacturers would be required to re-register a particular product. Effective administration would require a continued outlay of scarce resources to ensure that the registrations are accurate and up to date.

Setting up and maintaining this registration program in the Department of Commerce would entail a substantial commitment of resources and personnel. Departmental personnel would have to be diverted from the essential work they now perform in helping to promote U.S. exports.

Although H.R. 3342 would authorize a fee to be charged to manufacturers to cover the cost of registration, maintaining the phone line, responding to inquiries, and publicizing the hot line, such fee could potentially be prohibitive for manufacturers, especially for small businesses, given the high cost of administering this program effectively. In addition, companies, both large and small, would be forced to set up elaborate record keeping system to track ever changing input sources for their various product lines. The end result could be that manufacturers would forego using the made in America label altogether and U.S. consumers would have even less information than now available. Alternatively, any registration fees would be passed on to the consumer, raising the price of the product and possibly lowering that product's competitiveness with imports.

The legislation also raises a disturbing possibility that the program could be viewed as a U.S. government stamp of approval. The average consumer might consider inclusion of a product in a government-run hotline amounts to an official government imprimatur to a product. Consumers will not know that the Government has not investigated or approved the product's quality, safety, efficacy, etc.

In conclusion, for the reasons I have stated, the Department of Commerce does not support H.R. 3342. We appreciate your, as well as Congressman Traficant's, continued and unwavering support for U.S.-made products. Our work at the Department of Commerce to promote U.S. goods and services shares the same goal of ensuring a healthy, growing economy with good, high paying jobs for Americans. We look forward to working with you, Madam Chairwoman, and the other members of the Committee to advance these goals. I would be pleased to answer any questions that you may have.

Mrs. COLLINS. Thank you very much, Mr. Chung.

Before I begin my questions, let me say that the record is open so that members who did not give their opening statements can submit their opening statements, and they will be placed at the appropriate point in the record.

Now, Mr. Chung, the bill we are considering is designed to promote the purchases of American-made products by consumers here in the domestic U.S. market. Yet you say your job is to coordinate programs that promote exports of American goods and services.

Why were you chosen to testify on this legislation? What is the relationship between the requirements of this bill and the activities of the Office of Export Promotion Coordination of which you are the Director?

Mr. CHUNG. That is actually a good question and I am not sure whether I have a very good answer to that. I was asked by my supervisor, who is the Assistant Secretary for Trade Development, to testify this morning.

I don't know all the details as to how it got from the Secretary's Office through the Under Secretary's Office through the Assistant Secretary's Office and then to me.

As you know, we really have very little to do with any kind of labeling programs, so there is really no expert within the Commerce Department as we could determine to testify on this issue, so I am here.

Mrs. COLLINS. Well, let me ask you this question then. What agency within the Department of Commerce would you expect to be given responsibility for carrying out the provisions of this bill if it were to pass?

Mr. CHUNG. That is another interesting question. Again, I am not sure whether I have an answer to that. We have several agencies within the Department, International Trade Administration is one of several agencies, and if this bill does pass and if that responsibility for running the program is imposed on the Department, the Department will have to make a decision on that.

Mrs. COLLINS. Well, based on the assumption that there may be some kind of bill passed, would you ask someone in your Department or in the Department of Commerce to do a hypothetical and tell us which office might be involved in such an undertaking?

Mr. CHUNG. Would you like a written response to that question?

Mrs. COLLINS. Yes, I would, within 5 working days, please.

Mr. CHUNG. We will try to do that.

Mrs. COLLINS. Thank you very much.

In your statement, in your oral statement as well, there was a great discussion about labeling, and in your statement you say that the—I am quoting now, your written statement you say: "The United States manufacturers of goods that qualify as U.S. goods under the rules-of-origin in a foreign market but that do not qualify for a 'Made in America' labeling under this proposal could also lose a potential business benefit of such a label advertising the American quality of the product." End quote.

Now, I am not sure I understand what you are talking about. There is no labeling requirement in this bill at all. Instead, there is only a provision which allows manufacturers to put American-made products on a list at the Commerce Department and the

Commerce Department would give consumers access to that list. So I am going to ask you to explain how this bill would cause U.S. manufacturers of goods that qualify as U.S. goods under the rules-of-origin in a foreign market to lose the benefit of such a label?

Mr. CHUNG. We understand the bill as requiring a label that if you were going to be registering your product, one's product with the Commerce Department under the 1-800 number, that we assumed that product would bear a "Made in America" label. So with that assumption, that is the assumption under which that was—that statement was——

Mrs. COLLINS. There is no wording at all in this bill about a label, none whatsoever.

Mr. CHUNG. Let me consult with my general counsel.

Mrs. COLLINS. Of course.

Mr. CHUNG. I believe we were looking at this bill as well as the crime bill provision which does require a labeling and——

Mrs. COLLINS. They are not the same.

Mr. CHUNG. They are not the same and then we now have a clarification.

Mrs. COLLINS. Thank you.

Mr. CHUNG. Thank you.

Mrs. COLLINS. I understand that the Commerce Department doesn't have the same responsibilities for country-of-origin labeling that the Customs and the Federal Trade Commission have. I think you explained some of that.

However, this bill does not require the Commerce Department to investigate whether the products that are manufacturers on that list are actually made in America. As I understand it now, and I asked Mr. Traficant that question, too, so therefore do you agree that the Department would not have to independently certify or validate manufacturer's claims under this bill?

Mr. CHUNG. As we understand it, there doesn't seem to be that specific requirement, but then you may be relying on everyone to be telling truthfully when they sign whatever statement that they may be expected to sign, that their product is made in America to be telling the truth.

Mrs. COLLINS. Well, then Congressman Traficant said if, in fact, a consumer discovered for him or herself that this were not—that this was not the case, then that consumer could bring a claim and then once that claim was brought, the Commerce Department would not have to bring the claim, would not have to do an investigation. The consumer could then bring the claim, and it is at that point that something would kick in.

Mr. CHUNG. But somebody has to do the investigation at that point in time as to the truth of the claim. And I believe that Congressman Traficant mentioned that maybe FTC should do it. But then you are kind of dividing the jurisdiction here. You are asking the Commerce Department to maintain and operate the toll-free line and you are giving the money to the Commerce Department to do so. You are not giving any additional resources for the FTC to do the enforcement.

Mrs. COLLINS. But he wouldn't have to do it for the list. For the list, nothing would have to be done. The manufacturer, as I understand it, would have to call up the Commerce Department and say:

List my product. And as he explained it, a form would be sent out, he wants this thing listed and he says on here, on this piece of paper, my product is made in America, 50 percent standard, and all this kind of different stuff that Traficant explained.

Once that is done, it would be listed on the hotline or the telephone number, whatever they think it is going to be called, and that is all that Commerce would have to do. Then if someone called and said: Is this product, this particular product on your list? The person at Commerce would say, "yes" or "no" and that would be the end of it. Commerce does nothing else.

Mr. CHUNG. I understand.

Mrs. COLLINS. OK, thank you.

Mr. Greenwood.

Mr. GREENWOOD. Thank you, Madam Chairwoman.

Good morning, Mr. Chung.

Mr. CHUNG. Good morning.

Mr. GREENWOOD. You indicated earlier that you weren't quite sure why you were designated to come over here and deliver the bad news to the members of this committee.

Mr. CHUNG. I was asked to go, so I am here.

Mr. GREENWOOD. I understand that. My questions have to do with how the Commerce Department's position was determined on this issue. Was it left to you to determine?

Mr. CHUNG. No, sir.

Mr. GREENWOOD. You are delivering the testimony. Who determined in Commerce that the Department didn't support this proposal? Who prepared the testimony?

Mr. CHUNG. The testimony went through several layers of review, both within the International Trade Administration, as well as the Office of General Counsel for the Department. So this is the Department's view.

Mr. GREENWOOD. Was the Secretary of Commerce involved in developing the administration's position on this?

Mr. CHUNG. Not him personally, I don't believe, but his staff, his counsel and his Congressional people and myself and others were involved.

Mr. GREENWOOD. How much analysis did the Department put into determining how burdensome this responsibility could be? I share the Department's view that this could be an enormously burdensome task. Was there an effort made to count eligible products and estimate full-time equivalent staffers that it would take to answer "X" number of telephone lines?

Mr. CHUNG. The answer to that is partly yes, partly no. We didn't count the number of products. I wouldn't even know where to begin in that effort. But we did try to come up with some hypothetical situation of having to answer so many calls a week, setting up a database and things of that nature. And I would say, the fairly conservative estimate indicated that it would cost at least $3 million a year to be operate a program of any size.

Mr. GREENWOOD. That doesn't incorporate any responsibilities you might have to enforce fraudulently made claims.

Mr. CHUNG. That is correct.

Mr. GREENWOOD. Investigate claims that may be valid.

Mr. CHUNG. That is correct. That would be too conjectural at this point because we really don't have any idea of how many people will not be truthful in their applications and how many people will bring that to the attention of whoever the authorities may be that will be charged with the responsibility for enforcement. So $3 million is really guesswork.

Mr. GREENWOOD. Was that based on a specific number of employees?

Mr. CHUNG. Yes.

Mr. GREENWOOD. What was that number?

Mr. CHUNG. That was based upon handling 3,000 calls a week with a total of 27 employees and we came up with a minimum budgets of $3.6 million.

Mr. GREENWOOD. Have you shared the sheet that you are reading from which outlines your calculation with the committee? Does the committee staff have that?

Mr. CHUNG. I don't believe so.

Mr. GREENWOOD. Would you submit it with your——

Mr. CHUNG. It was so conjectural that I wasn't really sure it would be that useful. But if you wish to have it be part of the record, we will admit it.

Mr. GREENWOOD. Some conjecture may be better than no conjecture.

At a recent meeting with committee staff, FTC staff estimated the potential cost of enforcement to be, quote, "astronomical." Do you agree with that assessment?

Mr. CHUNG. Well, I would have to defer to their views on that because they are really the enforcement experts and Commerce really doesn't have much of any experience in that regard.

Mr. GREENWOOD. Has the Department estimated the cost of installing the toll-free telephone lines and maintaining them?

Mr. CHUNG. Not separately, but that is part of the $3.6 million.

Mr. GREENWOOD. So that is incorporated in the operating costs?

Mr. CHUNG. Yes, sir.

Mr. GREENWOOD. I had suggested to Mr. Traficant that if his idea is as valuable to American manufacturers and producers as he claims it to be, then perhaps it should be funded with private dollars from those very same manufacturers, rather than public dollars. He was open to the notion that perhaps we could fund this with private dollars and no government employees. Can you envision this whole process being carried out by an association of "Made in U.S.A." manufacturers with some sort of official link to the Department of Commerce for oversight responsibilities that might lessen the drain on Commerce resources but still give the imprimatur of the Federal Government to the project?

Mr. CHUNG. That is certainly a possibility, but I am not sure whether I am authorized at this point to authoritatively answer that question.

Mr. GREENWOOD. OK.

Thank you very much, Madam Chairwoman.

Mrs. COLLINS. Thank you, Mr. Chung, for appearing before us. We appreciate your testimony and we will be in touch with you. We may have some other questions. When they are received, we would appreciate it if we could have responses come back to us within 5 workings days.

Mr. CHUNG. We will do that.

Mrs. COLLINS. The hearing is adjourned.

[Whereupon, at 11:15 a.m., the hearing was adjourned.]

[The following letter was received for the record:]

UNITED STATES DEPARTMENT OF COMMERCE
International Trade Administration
Washington, D.C. 20230

JUN 7 1994

The Honorable Cardiss Collins
House of Representatives
Washington, D.C. 20515

Dear Congresswoman Collins:

Thank you for the opportunity to appear before your Subcommittee to testify on H.R. 3342. I deeply appreciate your courtesy and your attention to this issue.

I am enclosing the written answers to the follow-up questions asked of me when I testified before your Subcommittee on May 19, 1994. As you recall, I was asked which bureau within the Department of Commerce would have responsibility for implementing the "Made in America" hotline and what the projected cost of the program might be. The enclosed information has been approved by officials within the Department of Commerce and the Office of Management and Budget. It will be helpful to the Committee as it continues to review H.R. 3342.

If you would like additional information about the Department's position on this legislation, please do not hesitate to contact the International Trade Administration's Office of Legislative and Intergovernmental Affairs at (202) 482-3015. I will be working closely with this office to ensure that your concerns are addressed in a timely manner.

Sincerely,

T. S. Chung

T.S. Chung

QUESTION: If H.R. 3342 becomes law, where in the Department of Commerce would you place the program?

ANSWER: We are unable to say at this time exactly where in the Department we would place such a program. None of the agencies within the Department currently have any responsibilities relating to "Made in America" labeling or country of origin requirements, nor do the current mandates of the agencies lend themselves to taking on a new program such as that contemplated by H.R. 3342. It is possible that the Department would set up a separate office to administer the registration process for companies seeking to list their products on the hotline, and toll **free hotline and commitant enforcement procedures to effectively monitor the hotline**

QUESTION: How much will it cost to operate the toll-free Hot Line called for in H.R.3342?

ANSWER:

One of the primary reasons for the Department of Commerce's opposition to H.R. 3342 is the costly, new bureaucracy that would be required if it were enacted. Determining an accurate estimate of the costs to implement the toll-free hotline is difficult given the number of variables and questions raised by the bill. In addition, the Department of Commerce's International Trade Administration (ITA) has no experience in administering the kind of program envisioned in H.R. 3342. Consequently, ITA must make assumptions, which may or may not turn out to be correct, in order to calculate cost estimates. The tentative figures cited in the Hearing of May 19 were initial estimates developed at the staff level, without opportunity for higher level clearance within the Commerce or OMB.

Administrative overhead and start up expenses required to create a new office would, at the very minimum, include; a mix of employees, office space and equipment, and other items, e.g. training, equipment repair, advertising to both consumers and manufacturers, and accounting costs related to product registrations. Estimating the operational costs also depends significantly on the Department's ability to accurately anticipate the number of products registered, and the numbér of telephone calls from consumers.

We assume that charges to manufacturers would be assessed for each product that is registered, and that the user fee would be charged annually for each product registered. It is assumed that an additional fee would be charged for updating registered products.

Verification would be critical to the integrity and overall success of the program. Reliable verification of claims made by manufacturers would provide consumers with confidence that the hotline correctly identifies products as made in America. The lack of verification, and the absence of any enforcement mechanism would ultimately cost the U.S. taxpayers an even larger sum over the long term. The U.S. **taxpayer will be forced to pay for investigations and the prosecution of suspected offenders which could have been reduced if a reliable verification and enforcement mechanism existed in the first place.**

**Commerce estimates the** first year cost for start-up (personnel, equipment, etc.), program promotion, product registration and verification, accounting, and operation of the 1-800 telephone system to be as shown below.

**Estimated Costs and Full Time Personnel**

| | Product Registrations and Verifications | | |
|---|---|---|---|
| **Incoming Calls/Week** | 50,000 | 100,000 | 200,000 |
| 1,200 | $3,566,000/26FTE | $4,056,000/35FTE | $4,982,000/51FTE |
| 3,000 | 4,361,000/40FTE | 4,851,000/49FTE | 5,777,000/65FTE |
| 5,000 | 7,639,000/52FTE | 8,129,000/61FTE | 9,055,000/77FTE |

These **figures do not include the cost of enforcement. Under section** 3 **of the bill, violators would be subject to prosecution by the Federal Trade Commission under section 5 of the Federal Trade Commission** Act.

**It is not clear who would enforce the prohibition against Government procurement also** contained in section 3.

The Department would be unable initially to fund this activity from registration fees because all start-up costs would accrue prior to collection of any fees. The Department has neither the funding nor FTE allocated in its FY 1995 budget proposal to cover these costs.

○